BRITISH POETS
of the NINETEENTH CENTURY

POEMS BY

WORDSWORTH, COLERIDGE, SCOTT, BYRON, SHELLEY, KEATS,
LANDOR, TENNYSON, ELIZABETH BARRETT BROWNING,
ROBERT BROWNING, FITZGERALD, CLOUGH, ARNOLD,
DANTE GABRIEL ROSSETTI, CHRISTINA ROSSETTI,
MORRIS, SWINBURNE, DOBSON, HENLEY, KIPLING,
HOUSMAN

EDITED WITH REFERENCE LISTS AND NOTES

BY

CURTIS HIDDEN PAGE, Ph.D.

PROFESSOR OF ENGLISH IN
DARTMOUTH COLLEGE

NEW EDITION

BY

STITH THOMPSON, Ph.D.

PROFESSOR OF ENGLISH IN
INDIANA UNIVERSITY

PART TWO: TENNYSON TO HOUSMAN

BENJ. H. SANBORN & CO.

CHICAGO   NEW YORK   BOSTON

1936

To M. E. H.

To M. L. H.

PREFACE

1904

This volume makes no attempt to do what has already been so excellently done in Mr. Stedman's *Victorian Anthology*, Ward's *English Poets*, and other similar collections. It is not a new Anthology of nineteenth century poetry. Instead of giving a few "gems," or "flowers," from each one of several hundred authors, it includes only the fifteen chief poets of the century. From each one of these, however, it attempts to give a full and adequate selection, sufficient really to represent the man and his work.

The book has been planned, primarily, to give in one volume all the material which should be in the hands of the student for a College or University course on the British poets of the nineteenth century. I have therefore tried to include, first, all the poems which would be given as prescribed reading in such a course; and, second, a thorough guide to the use of a well-equipped college or public library, in connection with that reading. I hope the book may also be found useful for more general courses on English Literature, for which there is no other collection covering exactly this part of the field; and for any reader who wishes to possess in one volume the best work of the chief nineteenth century poets — "Infinite riches in a little room."

The selections are very full, and for the most part consist of complete poems. They are designed both to give all the best of each poet's work, and also (except for Mrs. Browning) to give some representation of each important period and class of his work. Long poems are usually given entire, and space has been found for Byron's *Manfred*, Shelley's *Prometheus Unbound*, Scott's *Marmion*, Coleridge's *Ancient Mariner* and *Christabel*, Keats' *Hyperion*, Tennyson's *Guinevere* and *Morte d'Arthur*, Browning's *Pippa Passes*, Mrs. Browning's *Sonnets from the Portuguese*, Arnold's *Sohrab and Rustum*, Morris's *Atalanta's Race*, etc., etc. In general, extracts from long poems are not given, except in the case of single cantos which are complete in themselves, like the last two cantos of *Childe Harold;* or lyrics, such as the songs from Tennyson's dramas, or the Hymns to Pan and Diana in Keats' *Endymion*, which, when detached, make perfect and independent poems. An exception has been made in the case of Byron's masterwork, *Don Juan*, which of course could not be given in full, and which has been represented by long passages.

The amount of space given to an author does not necessarily correspond with his relative importance or rank as a poet. Some authors can best be represented by their shorter poems, while others — Scott, for instance, and William Morris — could not be fairly represented at all unless one of their longer poems were given. Browning and Byron could not be represented without some complete example of their poems in dramatic form, while Tennyson's drama does not hold the same relative importance in his work. Byron, in particular, cannot really be known except through his longer poems; some example must necessarily be given of the series of Oriental Romances, which, with *Childe Harold*, won him his early fame; at least one Canto of *Childe Harold* must be given complete; an example of the great Satires must be known in the *Vision of Judgment;* and finally the whole man is summed up in the different aspects of *Don Juan*. Wordsworth, on the other hand, has less space than poets of inferior rank; but he is represented by a hundred complete poems, the largest number given for any author.

The selection of shorter poems has been made generously inclusive. For Browning, more than two-thirds of the *Dramatic Lyrics*, and more than half of the *Dramatic Romances* and *Men and Women*, as well as representative poems from the other collections, are given. For Keats, the entire contents (except one poem) of the volume of 1820 is given, as well as full representation of his earlier volumes and of the posthumous poems. I have included nearly eighty poems from Landor, and hope that this — I think the first — representative selection from his verse may serve to make his work as a poet more familiarly known, in the sheer beauty of its simplicity and condensation. No apology need be made, I hope, for the extent of the Shelley selections, since his *Alastor, Lines Written among the Euganean Hills, Epipsychidion, The Sensitive Plant, Adonais*, etc., as well as the *Prometheus Unbound*, make his work take a large amount of space in proportion to the number of titles. For Rossetti, I have given more than two-thirds of the sonnets from the *House of Life*, as well as *Sister Helen, The Stream's Secret, Love's Nocturn, The Burden of Nineveh, The King's Tragedy*, and some thirty or forty of the shorter poems. I hope that the space devoted to him will be found to represent a true judgment of his great permanent value as a poet; and that the same will be true of the still larger amount of space given to the poet most different from him, Matthew Arnold.

A principal feature of the volume is the classified *Reference Lists*. I have tried to indicate, for each poet, the standard editions, other important editions, the best one-volume editions, the standard biography, the best brief biography, and all the important essays. The critical essays are usually classed in two paragraphs, and, throughout, the most important books or essays are indicated by asterisks.

The Notes have been made as few and brief as possible; and critical comment, except that of the poet himself, or, in a few cases, of other poets, has been excluded from them. They give only essential *facts* regarding the poems, or comment and explanation added by the poet himself.

The poems are arranged in chronological order under each author, according to the dates of writing when these are known, and in other cases according to the dates of publication. The dates are given after each poem, dates of writing being indicated by italic figures, and dates of publication by upright figures.

It is a pleasure to acknowledge the ready generosity with which critics and teachers have given their help in making the selections. My thanks are due, in particular, to Mr. Paul E. More of the *New York Evening Post*, to Professor Stoddard of New York University, Professor Trent and Professor Odell of Columbia University, Professor Baker and Professor Sykes of Teachers' College, Professor van Dyke of Princeton, and Professor Mott of the College of the City of New York.

It can hardly be hoped that such a book as this will be entirely free from errors, especially in the reference lists and dates. Any corrections will be gratefully received. Most of the proof has been carefully read three times, but — as my friend Ronsard hath said — *Tu excuseras les fautes de l'imprimeur, car tous les yeux d'Argus n'y verraient assez clair.*

CURTIS HIDDEN PAGE

COLUMBIA UNIVERSITY
  September, 1904

PREFACE
1910

IN the present edition a number of typographical errors have been corrected, the text and dates of some poems have been verified by comparison with more authoritative editions than were available when the book was first published, an Index of First Lines has been added to the Author-Index and Title-Index, and the Reference Lists have been thoroughly revised and brought up to date. I am under obligation to several friends who have sent me corrections and especially suggestions for the improvement of the Reference Lists: in particular to Professor Lane Cooper, Professor Frank E. Farley, Miss Henriette E. Moore, Professor A. B. Milford, Professor Richard Jones, and Professor Charles W. Hodell; and I take this opportunity to thank the many other teachers who have written me concerning their use of the book. It is a pleasure to know that the general plan and method of the book, and of the Reference Lists, have been found helpful; and though these have been only too generously flattered by imitation, it is also a pleasure to note that no similar collection has ventured to include so much as one-third the material offered by the present volume.

C. H. P.

  September, 1910

PREFACE TO THE NEW EDITION
1929

THE present revision of *British Poets of the Nineteenth Century* has been carried out with the advice of Professor Page in an attempt to render it still more useful to its wide range of readers and students. The original plan remains unchanged: to give in attractive form, with ample critical help, abundant selections from the work of the truly outstanding British poets of the Nineteenth Century.

With minor exceptions all the poems of the first edition have been retained. A few poems of Clough and Dante Gabriel Rossetti, Scott's *Marmion,* and some of Mrs. Browning's *Sonnets from the Portuguese* are the only excisions. The omission of a few of Mrs. Browning's sonnets has given opportunity for the inclusion of a representative

group of her miscellaneous poems. Material additions have also been made to the
selections from Wordsworth and from Tennyson.

On the same generous scale as with the original fifteen poets in the collection, works
of six other writers have been added, and the scope of the book thus extended to the
end of the century. The poets appearing for the first time in this edition are FitzGerald,
Christina Rossetti, Dobson, Henley, Kipling, and Housman.

The reference lists have been brought down to date and new lists have been provided
for the poets added. So rapidly have critical works dealing with the poets of this
collection appeared in the past two decades that in many cases the reference lists are
more than twice the length of those in the revision of 1910. It is hoped that these
revised lists may prove especially helpful.

The entire book has been reset in a new form, so that although a very substantial
increase has been made in the number of poems the pages may be pleasant to read and
the book easy to carry.

Page's *British Poets of the Nineteenth Century* has long occupied a unique position
in its field. No higher goal could be set for the revision than to carry on with renewed
vigor this fine tradition of service to students and lovers of poetry.

Acknowledgment is made to Mr. Rudyard Kipling, to A. P. Watt & Son,
English agents for Rudyard Kipling, and to Doubleday, Doran and Company, Inc.,
American publishers, for permission to use the following poems: "The Ballad of East
and West" from *Barrack Room Ballads*, copyright 1892 and 1899 by Rudyard Kipling;
"Prelude to Departmental Ditties," copyright 1899 by Rudyard Kipling; "Danny
Deever" from *Barrack Room Ballads*, copyright 1892 and 1899 by Rudyard Kipling;
"Tommy" from *Barrack Room Ballads*, copyright 1892 and 1899 by Rudyard Kipling;
"Gunga Din" from *Barrack Room Ballads*, copyright 1892 and 1899 by Rudyard
Kipling; "Mandalay" from *Barrack Room Ballads*, copyright 1892 and 1899 by
Rudyard Kipling; "When Earth's Last Picture Is Painted" from *L'Envoi*, copy-
right 1892 by Rudyard Kipling; "In the Neolithic Age," copyright 1893 by Rud-
yard Kipling; "A Song of the English," copyright 1909 by Rudyard Kipling; "The
King," copyright 1899 by Rudyard Kipling; "The Song of the Banjo" from *The
Seven Seas*, copyright 1893, 1894, 1896, 1905 by Rudyard Kipling; "The 'Mary
Gloster'" from *The Seven Seas*, copyright 1893, 1894, 1896, 1905 by Rudyard Kipling;
"The Ladies" from *The Seven Seas*, copyright 1893, 1894, 1896, 1905 by Rudyard
Kipling; "Recessional" from *The Collected Verse*, copyright 1907, 1912 by Rudyard
Kipling; "The White Man's Burden," copyright 1899 by Rudyard Kipling; "M. I.,"
copyright 1901 by Rudyard Kipling; "The Islanders," copyright 1901 by Rudyard
Kipling; "Chant-Pagan" from *The Five Nations*, copyright 1903 by Rudyard Kipling;
"Boots" from *The Five Nations*, copyright 1903 by Rudyard Kipling; "If —," copy-
right 1910 by Rudyard Kipling; "The Female of the Species," copyright 1911 by
Rudyard Kipling.

STITH THOMPSON

INDIANA UNIVERSITY
May, 1929

TABLE OF CONTENTS[1]

TENNYSON

[1] The poems of each author are arranged in chronological order. Exact dates will be found at the end of each poem.

ix

TENNYSON

LIST OF REFERENCES

EDITIONS

*COMPLETE WORKS, 6 volumes, annotated by Alfred Lord Tennyson, edited by Hallam Lord Tennyson, Macmillan, 1908 (Eversley Edition). — COMPLETE WORKS, with LIFE, 10 volumes, Macmillan, 1899. — WORKS, 7 volumes, Houghton Mifflin, 1904 (New Riverside Edition). — POETICAL AND DRAMATIC WORKS, 3 volumes, Houghton Mifflin, 1906 (New Popular Edition). — WORKS, 10 volumes, edited by Eugene Parsons, Crowell, 1907 (Farringford Edition). — COMPLETE WORKS, 1 volume, Macmillan, 1893 (Globe Edition). — *POETICAL AND DRAMATIC WORKS, 1 volume, edited by W. J. Rolfe, Houghton Mifflin, 1898 (Cambridge Edition). — WORKS, 1 volume, 1907 (Oxford Edition). — LYRICAL POEMS, selected by F. T. Palgrave, Macmillan, 1900 (Golden Treasury Series). — POEMS, chosen and edited by Henry van Dyke, Ginn, 1903. — POEMS, 1830–1865, edited by T. H. Warren, Clarendon Press, 1911.

BIOGRAPHY

*TENNYSON (Hallam), Alfred, Lord Tennyson, a Memoir, 2 volumes, 1897; new edition, 1 volume, 1905 (the standard biography). — HORTON (R. F.), Life of Tennyson, 1900. — LANG (A.), Alfred Tennyson, 1901 (Modern English Writers). — LYALL (A. C.), Tennyson, 1902 (English Men of Letters Series). — CHESTERTON (G. K.), Tennyson, 1904 (Bookman Biographies). — WAUGH (Arthur), Life of Tennyson, 1893. *BENSON (A. C.), Alfred Tennyson, 1904 (Little Biographies). — CUTHBERTSON (E. J.), Tennyson, the Story of his Life, 1898. — LOUNSBURY (T. R.), The Life and Times of Tennyson, 1915. — TENNYSON (Hallam), Tennyson and His Friends, 1912. — THOMAS (E.), A Literary Pilgrim in England: Tennyson, 1917. — WATSON (A.), Tennyson, 1913. — WOODBERRY (G. E.), Studies of a Litterateur: Tennyson, 1921. — *See also:* combined biographies and criticisms, listed under LATER CRITICISM, by the following authors: Alden, Fausset, Ker, Nicholson, and Willocks.

REMINISCENCES AND EARLY CRITICISM

*HALLAM (A. H.), Literary Remains: On Some Characteristics of Modern Poetry and on the Lyrical Poems of Alfred Tennyson (from Englishman's Magazine, August, 1831). — WILSON (John), Essays: Tennyson's Poems (essay of 1832). — [LOCKHART (J. G.)], Tennyson's Poems (in Quarterly Review, April, 1833). — MILL (J. S.), Early Essays: Tennyson's Poems (from London Review, July, 1835). — STERLING (John), Essays and Tales: Tennyson's Poems (1842). — SPEDDING (James), Reviews: Tennyson's Poems (1843). — HORNE (R. H.), A New Spirit of the Age, 1844. — KINGSLEY (C.), Miscellanies, 1850. — MILSAND (J.), La Poésie anglaise depuis Lord Byron (in Revue des Deux Mondes, July 15, 1851). — *BRIMLEY (G.), Essays: Tennyson's Poems (from Cambridge Essays, 1855). — MASSEY (Gerald), Tennyson and His Poetry, 1855. — *ROSCOE (W. C.), Poems and Essays, Vol. II, 1860. — *TAINE (H.), Histoire de la littérature anglaise, 1863; English translation, 1871. — *BAGEHOT (W.), Literary Studies, Vol. II, 1879; Wordsworth, Tennyson, and Browning (essay of 1864). — FIELDS (J. T.), Yesterdays with Authors, 1872. — FIELDS (Mrs. Annie), Authors and Friends, 1896. — *RITCHIE (Anne Thackeray), Records of Tennyson, Ruskin, Browning, 1892. — *NAPIER (G. S.), Homes and Haunts of Tennyson, 1892. — VAN DYKE (Henry), The Voice of Tennyson (in Century Magazine, January, 1893). — *KNOWLES (J.), Personal Reminiscences of Tennyson (in Nineteenth Century, January, 1893). — SYMONDS

(J. A.), Recollections of Tennyson (in Century Magazine, May, 1893). — RAWNSLEY
(H. D.), Memories of the Tennysons, 1900. — FRISWELL (Laura H.), In the Sixties and
Seventies, 1906. — ELLISON (Edith N.), A Child's Recollections of Tennyson, 1906. —
CONWAY (M. D.), Autobiography, 1907. — ARNOLD (W. H.), My Tennysons (in
Scribner's, May, 1922). — CORNISH (Mrs. W.), Personal Memories of the Tennysons
(in Living Age, May 13–27, 1922). — RAWNSLEY (H. D.), Personal Recollections of the
Tennysons (in Nineteenth Century, January, 1925).

LATER CRITICISM

BROOKE (S. A.), Tennyson, His Art and Relation to Modern Life, 1894. — CHESTER-
TON (G. K.), Twelve Types, 1902. — *DOWDEN (Edward), Studies in Literature : Mr.
Tennyson and Mr. Browning, 1878. — EVERETT (C. C.), Essays : Tennyson and Brown-
ing as Spiritual Forces, 1891. — *GATES (L. E.), Studies and Appreciations, 1900. —
GOSSE (E.), Questions at Issue : Tennyson — and After, 1893. — HARRISON (Frederic),
Tennyson, Ruskin, Mill, and Other Literary Estimates, 1899. — *HUTTON (R. H.),
Literary Essays, 1871, 1888. — HENLEY (W. E.), Views and Reviews, 1890. — MACKIE
(A.), Nature Knowledge in Modern Poetry, 1906. — MUSTARD (W. P.), Classical Echoes
in Tennyson, 1904. — MYERS (F. W. H.), Science and a Future Life, 1893 (essay of
1889). — PAYNE (W. M.), The Greater English Poets of the Nineteenth Century, 1907.
— ROBERTSON (J. M.), Essays towards a Critical Method, 1889. — *ROYCE (J.),
Studies of Good and Evil : Tennyson and Pessimism, 1898. — SAINTSBURY (G.), Cor-
rected Impressions, 1895. — SHAIRP (J. C.), Aspects of Poetry, 1881. — *STEDMAN
(E. C.), Victorian Poets, 1875, 1887. — STEPHEN (Leslie), Studies of a Biographer,
Vol. II, 1899. — *SWINBURNE (A. C.), Miscellanies : Tennyson and Musset, 1886. —
TRAILL (H. D.), Aspects of Tennyson (in Nineteenth Century, December, 1892.) —
*VAN DYKE (Henry), Poetry of Tennyson, 1889. — WALTERS (J. C.), Tennyson : Poet,
Philosopher, Idealist, 1893. — WARD (W. G.), Tennyson's Debt to His Environment,
1898. — WATTS-DUNTON (T.), Tennyson as a Nature Poet ; Tennyson and the Scientific
Movement (in Nineteenth Century, May, 1893, October, 1893). — WHITMAN (W.),
Democratic Vistas.

ADAMS (F.), Essays in Modernity, 1899. — AUSTIN (A.), The Bridling of Pegasus,
1910. — DIXON (W. M.), A Primer of Tennyson, 1896. — FAGUET (Émile), Centenary
of Tennyson (in Quarterly Review, April, 1909). — GORDON (William C.), Social Ideals
of Tennyson, 1906. — GLADSTONE (W. E.), Gleanings of Past Years (1859), 1879. —
HOWELLS (W. D.), My Literary Passions. — HUTTON (R. H.), Brief Literary Criticisms,
1906. — *KER (W. P.), Tennyson, 1910. — LUCE (M.), A Handbook to the Works of
Tennyson, 1895. — MASTERMAN, Tennyson as a Religious Teacher, 1900. — PAYNE
(W. M.), Little Leaders, 1895. — PEARSON (C. W.), Literary and Biographical Essays,
1908. — PECK (H. T.), Studies in Several Literatures : The Lyrics of Tennyson, 1909.—
SLICER (T. R.), From Poet to Premier, 1909. — SNEATH (E. H.), The Mind of Tennyson,
1900. — STANLEY (H. M.), Essays on Literary Art, 1897. — TAYLOR (Bayard), Critical
Essays, 1880. — WARREN (T. H.), Essays of Poets and Poetry, 1909.

AINGER (A.), Lectures and Essays : The Death of Tennyson, 1905. — ALDEN (R. M.),
Alfred Tennyson, 1917. — BARERA (E.), A Critical Essay on the Works of Alfred,
Lord Tennyson, 1896. — BOAS (G.), Tennyson and Browning, 1925. — BRADLEY
(A. C.), The Reaction against Tennyson (in English Association Pamphlet No. 39). —
CHOISY (L. F.), Alfred Tennyson, son spiritualisme, sa personalité morale, 1912. —
CLARK (J. S.), A Study of English and American Poets : Tennyson, 1917. — DYBOSKI
(R.), Tennysons Sprache und Stil (in Wiener Beiträge zur Englischen Philologie, 1907).
— DRINKWATER (J.), Victorian Poetry, 1924. — FAUSSET (H. I.), Tennyson, a Modern
Portrait, 1923. — FLETCHER (R. H.), Tennyson and Browning, 1913. — GINGERICH
(S. F.), Wordsworth, Tennyson, and Browning, 1911. — GRIERSON (H. J. C.), The
Tennysons (in Cambridge History of English Literature, Vol. XIII). — GUNSAULUS
(F. W.), The Higher Ministries of Recent English Poetry, 1907. — GWINN (S. L.),
Tennyson, a Critical Study, 1899. — HUCKEL (O.), Through England with Tennyson,

1913. — LAYARD (G. S.), Tennyson and His Pre-Raphaelite Illustrators, 1894. — LOCKYER (Sir J. N.), Tennyson as a Student and Poet of Nature, 1910. — MACKAIL (J. W.), Lectures on Greek Poetry: Theocritus and Tennyson, 1911; Studies of English Poets, 1926. — MEYNELL (Alice), Tennyson (in Dublin Review, January, 1910). — MORE (P. E.), Tennyson, Poet of National Life (in Shelburne Essays, seventh series). — NICOLSON (H. G.), Tennyson, 1923. — NITCHIE (E.), Vergil and the English Poets: Tennyson and the Victorians, 1919. — NOYES (A.), Some Aspects of Modern Poetry: Tennyson and Some Recent Critics, 1924. — PALMER (G. H.), Formative Types in English Poetry, 1918. — PYRE (J. F. A.), The Formation of Tennyson's Style, 1921. — ROBINSON (Edna M.), Tennyson's Use of the Bible, 1917. — ROZ (F.), Tennyson, 1911. — STORK (C. W.), Heine and Tennyson (in Haverford Essays, 1909). — WARD (W.), Tennyson's Religious Poetry (in Dublin Review, October, 1909). — WATSON (A.), Tennyson, 1913 (The People's Books). — WEATHERHEAD (L. D.), Tennyson's Afterworld (in London Quarterly Review, October, 1925). — WILLOCKS (M. P.), Tennyson (in English Review, February, 1923).

IN MEMORIAM. — *Editions:* — TENNYSON: In Memoriam, annotated by the Author, 1906. — BEECHING (H. C.), In Memoriam, with an analysis and notes, 1900. — MANSFORD (C.), In Memoriam, 1903. — ROLFE (W. J.), In Memoriam, edited, with notes, etc., 1895. — SQUIRES (Vernon P.), In Memoriam, edited, with introduction and notes, 1906. — *Commentary:* — BRADLEY (A. C.), Commentary on In Memoriam. — CHAPMAN (Elizabeth R.), A Companion to In Memoriam, 1888 (recommended by Tennyson). — DAVIDSON (Thomas), Prolegomena to In Memoriam, 1889. — GATTY (A.), Key to Tennyson's In Memoriam, 1881. — GENUNG (J. F.), Tennyson's In Memoriam, Its Purpose and its Structure, 1884. — JACOBS (J.), Tennyson and In Memoriam, 1892.

IDYLLS OF THE KING. — DHALEINE (L.), A Study of Tennyson's Idylls of the King, 1905. — GENUNG (J. F.), The Idylls and the Ages, 1907. — GURTEEN (S. H.), The Arthurian Epic, 1895. — HAMANN (Albert), An Essay on Tennyson's Idylls of the King, 1887. — *JONES (Richard), The Growth of the Idylls of the King, 1895. — *LITTLEDALE (H.), Essays on Tennyson's Idylls of the King, 1893. — MACCALLUM (M. W.), Tennyson's Idylls and Arthurian Story from the Sixteenth Century, 1894. — *MAYNADIER (H.), The Arthur of the English Poets, 1907. — NICOLL (W. R.) and WISE (T. J.), Literary Anecdotes of the Nineteenth Century: The Building of the Idylls, 1896. — PALLEN (Condé Bénoist), The Meaning of the Idylls, 1904. — WUELLENWEBER (W.), Ueber Tennyson's Königsidylle: The Coming of Arthur und ihre Quellen, 1889. — ELSDALE (H.), Studies in the Idylls, 1878.

TRIBUTES IN VERSE

WATSON (W.), *Lacrymæ Musarum; To Lord Tennyson; The Foresters. — *HUXLEY (T. H.), in Stedman's Victorian Anthology. — GILDER (R. W.), The Silence of Tennyson. — BOURDILLON (F. W.), Sursum Corda. — ALDRICH (T. B.),* Tennyson; "When from the tense chords . . . ," January, 1892. — *LONGFELLOW, Wapentake. — MACKAYE (Percy), Poems. — HUDSON (J.), Tennyson's Birthday (in Westminster Review, August, 1910). — VAN DYKE (Henry), Tennyson, 1892.

BIBLIOGRAPHY, ETC.

SHEPHERD (R. H.), Bibliography of Tennyson, 1896. — GROLIER CLUB, Chronological List of Tennyson's Works, 1897. — COLLINS, The Early Poems of Tennyson, with Bibliography and Various Readings, 1900. — DIXON (W. M.), A Primer of Tennyson, with Bibliography, 1896. — LUCE (Morton), Handbook to the Works of Tennyson, 1895. — PROVIDENCE PUBLIC LIBRARY, Tennyson Reference List (Monthly Bulletin, October, 1897). — LIVINGSTON (L. S.), Bibliography of the First Editions, 1901. — *WISE (T. J.), Bibliography of Tennyson, 1908. — BAKER (A. E.), A Concordance to the Poetical and Dramatic Works of Alfred, Lord Tennyson, 1914; A Tennyson Dictionary, 1916.

TENNYSON

CLARIBEL

A MELODY

WHERE Claribel low-lieth
  The breezes pause and die,
    Letting the rose-leaves fall;
But the solemn oak-tree sigheth,
Thick-leaved, ambrosial,
  With an ancient melody
  Of an inward agony,
Where Claribel low-lieth.

At eve the beetle boometh
  Athwart the thicket lone;
At noon the wild bee hummeth
  About the moss'd headstone:
At midnight the moon cometh,
  And looketh down alone.
Her song the lintwhite swelleth,
The clear-voiced mavis dwelleth,
  The callow throstle lispeth,
  The slumbrous wave outwelleth,
  The babbling runnel crispeth,
The hollow grot replieth
  Where Claribel low-lieth. 1830.

THE POET

THE poet in a golden clime was born,
  With golden stars above;
Dower'd with the hate of hate, the scorn
    of scorn,
  The love of love.

He saw thro' life and death, thro' good
    and ill,
  He saw thro' his own soul.
The marvel of the everlasting will,
  An open scroll,

Before him lay; with echoing feet he
    threaded
  The secretest walks of fame:
The viewless arrows of his thoughts were
    headed
  And wing'd with flame,

Like Indian reeds blown from his silver
    tongue,
  And so fierce a flight,
From Calpe unto Caucasus they sung,
  Filling with light

And vagrant melodies the winds which
    bore
  Them earthward till they lit;
Then, like the arrow-seeds of the field
    flower,
  The fruitful wit

Cleaving took root, and springing forth
    anew
  Where'er they fell, behold,
Like to the mother plant in semblance,
    grew
  A flower all gold,

And bravely furnish'd all abroad to fling
  The winged shafts of truth,
To throng with stately blooms the breath-
    ing spring
  Of Hope and Youth.

So many minds did gird their orbs with
    beams,
  Tho' one did fling the fire;
Heaven flow'd upon the soul in many
    dreams
  Of high desire.

Thus truth was multiplied on truth, the
    world
  Like one great garden show'd,
And thro' the wreaths of floating dark
    upcurl'd,
  Rare sunrise flow'd.

And Freedom rear'd in that august sun-
    rise
  Her beautiful bold brow,
When rites and forms before his burning
    eyes
  Melted like snow.

445

There was no blood upon her maiden
    robes
        Sunn'd by those orient skies;
But round about the circles of the globes
    Of her keen eyes

And in her raiment's hem was traced in
    flame
        WISDOM, a name to shake
All evil dreams of power — a sacred
    name.
        And when she spake,

Her words did gather thunder as they ran,
    And as the lightning to the thunder
Which follows it, riving the spirit of man,
    Making earth wonder,

So was their meaning to her words.   No
    sword
        Of wrath her right arm whirl'd,
But one poor poet's scroll, and with *his*
    word
        She shook the world.   1830.

MARIANA

"Mariana in the moated grange."
                Measure for Measure.

WITH blackest moss the flower-plots
    Were thickly crusted, one and all;
The rusted nails fell from the knots
    That held the pear to the gable-wall.
The broken sheds look'd sad and strange:
    Unlifted was the clinking latch;
    Weeded and worn the ancient thatch
Upon the lonely moated grange.
        She only said, "My life is dreary,
            He cometh not," she said;
        She said, "I am aweary, aweary,
            I would that I were dead!"

Her tears fell with the dews at even;
    Her tears fell ere the dews were dried;
She could not look on the sweet heaven,
    Either at morn or eventide.
After the flitting of the bats,
    When thickest dark did trance the sky,
    She drew her casement-curtain by,
And glanced athwart the glooming flats.
        She only said, "The night is dreary,
            He cometh not," she said;
        She said, "I am aweary, aweary,
            I would that I were dead!"

Upon the middle of the night,
    Waking she heard the night-fowl crow;
The cock sung out an hour ere light;
    From the dark fen the oxen's low
Came to her; without hope of change,
    In sleep she seem'd to walk forlorn,
    Till cold winds woke the gray-eyed
        morn
About the lonely moated grange.
        She only said, "The day is dreary,
            He cometh not," she said;
        She said, "I am aweary, aweary,
            I would that I were dead!"

About a stone-cast from the wall
    A sluice with blacken'd waters slept,
And o'er it many, round and small,
    The cluster'd marish-mosses crept.
Hard by a poplar shook alway,
    All silver-green with gnarled bark:
    For leagues no other tree did mark
The level waste, the rounding gray.
        She only said, "My life is dreary,
            He cometh not," she said;
        She said, "I am aweary, aweary,
            I would that I were dead!"

And ever when the moon was low,
    And the shrill winds were up and away,
In the white curtain, to and fro,
    She saw the gusty shadow sway.
But when the moon was very low,
    And wild winds bound within their cell,
    The shadow of the poplar fell
Upon her bed, across her brow.
        She only said, "The night is dreary,
            He cometh not," she said;
        She said, "I am aweary, aweary,
            I would that I were dead!"

All day within the dreamy house,
    The doors upon their hinges creak'd;
The blue fly sung in the pane; the mouse
    Behind the mouldering wainscot
        shriek'd,
Or from the crevice peer'd about.
    Old faces glimmer'd thro' the doors,
    Old footsteps trod the upper floors,
Old voices called her from without.
        She only said, "My life is dreary,
            He cometh not," she said;
        She said, "I am aweary, aweary,
            I would that I were dead!"

The sparrow's chirrup on the roof,
    The slow clock ticking, and the sound

Which to the wooing wind aloof
The poplar made, did all confound
Her sense; but most she loathed the hour
When the thick-moted sunbeam lay
Athwart the chambers, and the day
Was sloping toward his western bower.
Then said she, "I am very dreary,
He will not come," she said;
She wept, "I am aweary, aweary,
O God, that I were dead!"

1830, 1842.

THE MERMAN

I

WHO would be
A merman bold,
Sitting alone,
Singing alone
Under the sea,
With a crown of gold,
On a throne?

II

I would be a merman bold,
I would sit and sing the whole of the day;
I would fill the sea-halls with a voice of
power;
But at night I would roam abroad and
play
With the mermaids in and out of the
rocks,
Dressing their hair with the white sea-
flower;
And holding them back by their flowing
locks
I would kiss them often under the sea,
And kiss them again till they kiss'd me
Laughingly, laughingly;
And then we would wander away, away,
To the pale-green sea-groves straight and
high,
Chasing each other merrily.

III

There would be neither moon nor star;
But the wave would make music above us
afar —
Low thunder and light in the magic
night —
Neither moon nor star.
We would call aloud in the dreamy dells,
Call to each other and whoop and cry
All night, merrily, merrily.

They would pelt me with starry spangles
and shells,
Laughing and clapping their hands be-
tween,
All night, merrily, merrily,
But I would throw to them back in mine
Turkis and agate and almondine;
Then leaping out upon them unseen
I would kiss them often under the sea,
And kiss them again till they kiss'd me
Laughingly, laughingly.
O, what a happy life were mine
Under the hollow-hung ocean green!
Soft are the moss-beds under the sea;
We would live merrily, merrily.

1830, 1842.

THE MERMAID

I

WHO would be
A mermaid fair,
Singing alone,
Combing her hair
Under the sea,
In a golden curl
With a comb of pearl,
On a throne?

II

I would be a mermaid fair;
I would sing to myself the whole of the
day;
With a comb of pearl I would comb my
hair;
And still as I comb'd I would sing and say,
"Who is it loves me? who loves not me?"
I would comb my hair till my ringlets
would fall
Low adown, low adown,
From under my starry sea-bud crown
Low adown and around,
And I should look like a fountain of gold
Springing alone
With a shrill inner sound,
Over the throne
In the midst of the hall;
Till that great sea-snake under the sea
From his coiled sleeps in the central deeps
Would slowly trail himself sevenfold
Round the hall where I sate, and look in
at the gate
With his large calm eyes for the love of
me.

And all the mermen under the sea
Would feel their immortality
Die in their hearts for the love of me.

III

But at night I would wander away, away,
   I would fling on each side my low-flow-
      ing locks,
And lightly vault from the throne and play
    With the mermen in and out of the
      rocks;
We would run to and fro, and hide and
      seek,
    On the broad sea-wolds in the crimson
      shells,
Whose silvery spikes are nighest the sea.
But if any came near I would call, and
      shriek,
And adown the steep like a wave I would
      leap
    From the diamond-ledges that jut
      from the dells;
For I would not be kiss'd by all who would
      list
Of the bold merry mermen under the sea.
They would sue me, and woo me, and
      flatter me,
In the purple twilights under the sea;
But the king of them all would carry me,
Woo me, and win me, and marry me,
In the branching jaspers under the sea.
Then all the dry pied things that be
In the hueless mosses under the sea
Would curl round my silver feet silently,
All looking up for the love of me.
And if I should carol aloud, from aloft
All things that are forked, and horned,
      and soft
Would lean out from the hollow sphere of
      the sea,
All looking down for the love of me.
                1830, 1842.

THE LADY OF SHALOTT [1]

PART I

ON either side the river lie
Long fields of barley and of rye,
That clothe the wold and meet the sky;
And thro' the field the road runs by
    To many-tower'd Camelot;

[1] See the *Life of Tennyson*, by his Son, I, 116–117.

And up and down the people go,
Gazing where the lilies blow
Round an island there below,
    The island of Shalott.

Willows whiten, aspens quiver,
Little breezes dusk and shiver
Thro' the wave that runs for ever
By the island in the river
    Flowing down to Camelot.
Four gray walls, and four gray towers,
Overlook a space of flowers,
And the silent isle imbowers
    The Lady of Shalott.

By the margin, willow-veil'd,
Slide the heavy barges trail'd
By slow horses; and unhail'd
The shallop flitteth silken-sail'd
    Skimming down to Camelot;
But who hath seen her wave her hand?
Or at the casement seen her stand?
Or is she known in all the land,
    The Lady of Shalott?

Only reapers, reaping early
In among the bearded barley
Hear a song that echoes cheerly
From the river winding clearly,
    Down to tower'd Camelot;
And by the moon the reaper weary,
Piling sheaves in uplands airy,
Listening, whispers "'T is the fairy
    Lady of Shalott."

PART II

There she weaves by night and day
A magic web with colors gay.
She has heard a whisper say,
A curse is on her if she stay
    To look down to Camelot.
She knows not what the curse may be,
And so she weaveth steadily,
And little other care hath she,
    The Lady of Shalott.

And moving thro' a mirror clear
That hangs before her all the year,
Shadows of the world appear.
There she sees the highway near
    Winding down to Camelot;
There the river eddy whirls,
And there the surly village-churls,
And the red cloaks of market girls,
    Pass onward from Shalott.

Sometimes a troop of damsels glad,
An abbot on an ambling pad,
Sometimes a curly shepherd-lad,
Or long-hair'd page in crimson clad,
    Goes by to tower'd Camelot;
And sometimes thro' the mirror blue
The knights come riding two and two:
She hath no loyal knight and true,
    The Lady of Shalott.

But in her web she still delights
To weave the mirror's magic sights,
For often thro' the silent nights
A funeral, with plumes and lights
    And music, went to Camelot;
Or when the moon was overhead,
Came two young lovers lately wed:
"I am half sick of shadows," said
    The Lady of Shalott.

PART III

A bow-shot from her bower-eaves,
He rode between the barley-sheaves,
The sun came dazzling thro' the leaves,
And flamed upon the brazen greaves
    Of bold Sir Lancelot.
A red-cross knight for ever kneel'd
To a lady in his shield,
That sparkled on the yellow field,
    Beside remote Shalott.

To gemmy bridle glitter'd free,
Like to some branch of stars we see
Hung in the golden Galaxy.
The bridle bells rang merrily
    As he rode down to Camelot;
And from his blazon'd baldric slung
A mighty silver bugle hung,
And as he rode his armor rung,
    Beside remote Shalott.

All in the blue unclouded weather
Thick-jewell'd shone the saddle-leather,
The helmet and the helmet-feather
Burn'd like one burning flame together,
    As he rode down to Camelot;
As often thro' the purple night,
Below the starry clusters bright,
Some bearded meteor, trailing light,
    Moves over still Shalott.

His broad clear brow in sunlight glow'd;
On burnish'd hooves his war-horse trode;
From underneath his helmet flow'd
His coal-black curls as on he rode,
    As he rode down to Camelot.

From the bank and from the river
He flash'd into the crystal mirror,
"Tirra lirra," by the river
    Sang Sir Lancelot.

She left the web, she left the loom,
She made three paces thro' the room,
She saw the water-lily bloom,
She saw the helmet and the plume,
    She look'd down to Camelot.
Out flew the web and floated wide;
The mirror crack'd from side to side;
"The curse is come upon me," cried
    The Lady of Shalott.

PART IV

In the stormy east-wind straining,
The pale yellow woods were waning,
The broad stream in his banks complain-
    ing,
Heavily the low sky raining
    Over tower'd Camelot;
Down she came and found a boat
Beneath a willow left afloat,
And round about the prow she wrote
    The Lady of Shalott.

And down the river's dim expanse
Like some bold seër in a trance,
Seeing all his own mischance —
With a glassy countenance
    Did she look to Camelot.
And at the closing of the day
She loosed the chain, and down she lay;
The broad stream bore her far away,
    The Lady of Shalott.

Lying, robed in snowy white
That loosely flew to left and right —
The leaves upon her falling light —
Thro' the noises of the night
    She floated down to Camelot;
And as the boat-head wound along
The willowy hills and fields among,
They heard her singing her last song,
    The Lady of Shalott.

Heard a carol, mournful, holy,
Chanted loudly, chanted lowly,
Till her blood was frozen slowly
And her eyes were darken'd wholly
    Turn'd to tower'd Camelot.
For ere she reach'd upon the tide
The first house by the water-side,
Singing in her song she died,
    The Lady of Shalott.

Under tower and balcony,
By garden-wall and gallery,
A gleaming shape she floated by,
Dead-pale between the houses high,
    Silent into Camelot.
Out upon the wharfs they came.
Knight and burgher, lord and dame,
And round the prow they read her name,
    The Lady of Shalott.

Who is this? and what is here?
And in the lighted palace near
Died the sound of royal cheer,
And they cross'd themselves for fear,
    All the knights at Camelot:
But Lancelot mused a little space;
He said, "She has a lovely face;
God in his mercy lend her grace,
    The Lady of Shalott."
               1832, 1842.

SONG: THE MILLER'S DAUGHTER

IT is the miller's daughter,
    And she is grown so dear, so dear,
That I would be the jewel
    That trembles in her ear;
For hid in ringlets day and night,
I'd touch her neck so warm and white.

And I would be the girdle
    About her dainty dainty waist,
And her heart would beat against me,
    In sorrow and in rest;
And I should know if it beat right,
I'd clasp it round so close and tight.

And I would be the necklace,
    And all day long to fall and rise
Upon her balmy bosom,
    With her laughter or her sighs;
And I would lie so light, so light,
I scarce should be unclasp'd at night.
               1832.

ŒNONE

THERE lies a vale in Ida, lovelier
Than all the valleys of Ionian hills.
The swimming vapor slopes athwart the
    glen,
Puts forth an arm, and creeps from pine
    to pine,
And loiters, slowly drawn. On either
    hand

The lawns and meadow-ledges midway
    down
Hang rich in flowers, and far below them
    roars
The long brook falling thro' the cloven
    ravine
In cataract after cataract to the sea.
Behind the valley topmost Gargarus
Stands up and takes the morning; but
    in front
The gorges, opening wide apart, reveal
Troas and Ilion's column'd citadel,
The crown of Troas.
              Hither came at noon
Mournful Œnone, wandering forlorn
Of Paris, once her playmate on the hills.
Her cheek had lost the rose, and round
    her neck
Floated her hair or seem'd to float in rest.
She, leaning on a fragment twined with
    vine,
Sang to the stillness till the mountain-
    shade
Sloped downward to her seat from the
    upper cliff.

"O mother Ida, many-fountain'd Ida,
Dear mother Ida, harken ere I die.
For now the noonday quiet holds the hill;
The grasshopper is silent in the grass;
The lizard, with his shadow on the
    stone,
Rests like a shadow, and the winds are
    dead.
The purple flower droops, the golden bee
Is lily-cradled: I alone awake.
My eyes are full of tears, my heart of
    love,
My heart is breaking and my eyes are
    dim,
And I am all aweary of my life.

"O mother Ida, many-fountain'd Ida,
Dear mother Ida, harken ere I die.
Hear me, O earth, hear me, O hills, O
    caves
That house the cold crown'd snake! O
    mountain brooks,
I am the daughter of a River God,
Hear me, for I will speak, and build up
    all
My sorrow with my song, as yonder
    walls
Rose slowly to a music slowly breathed,
A cloud that gather'd shape; for it may
    be

That, while I speak of it, a little while
My heart may wander from its deeper
    woe.

"O mother Ida, many-fountain'd Ida,
Dear mother Ida, harken ere I die.
I waited underneath the dawning hills;
Aloft the mountain-lawn was dewy-dark,
And dewy-dark aloft the mountain-pine.
Beautiful Paris, evil-hearted Paris,
Leading a jet-black goat white-horn'd,
    white-hooved,
Came up from reedy Simois all alone.

"O mother Ida, harken ere I die.
Far off the torrent call'd me from the
    cleft;
Far up the solitary morning smote
The streaks of virgin snow. With down-
    dropt eyes
I sat alone; white-breasted like a star
Fronting the dawn he moved; a leopard
    skin
Droop'd from his shoulder, but his sunny
    hair
Cluster'd about his temples like a God's;
And his cheek brighten'd as the foam-bow
    brightens
When the wind blows the foam, and all
    my heart
Went forth to embrace him coming ere
    he came.

"Dear mother Ida, harken ere I die.
He smiled, and opening out his milk-
    white palm
Disclosed a fruit of pure Hesperian gold,
That smelt ambrosially, and while I
    look'd
And listen'd, the full-flowing river of
    speech
Came down upon my heart:
    'My own Œnone,
Beautiful-brow'd Œnone, my own soul,
Behold this fruit, whose gleaming rind
    ingraven
"For the most fair," would seem to award
    it thine,
As lovelier than whatever Oread haunt
The knolls of Ida, loveliest in all grace
Of movement, and the charm of married
    brows.'

"Dear mother Ida, harken ere I die.
He pressed the blossom of his lips to
    mine,

And added, 'This was cast upon the
    board.
When all the full-faced presence of the
    Gods
Ranged in the halls of Peleus; whereupon
Rose feud, with question unto whom
    'twere due;
But light-foot Iris brought it yester-eve,
Delivering, that to me, by common voice
Elected umpire, Herè comes to-day,
Pallas and Aphrodite, claiming each
This meed of fairest. Thou, within the
    cave
Behind yon whispering tuft of oldest
    pine,
Mayst well behold them unbeheld, un-
    heard
Hear all, and see thy Paris, judge of
    Gods.'

"Dear mother Ida, harken ere I die.
It was the deep midnoon; one silvery
    cloud
Had lost his way between the piny sides
Of this long glen. Then to the bower
    they came,
Naked they came to that smooth
    swarded bower,
And at their feet the crocus brake like
    fire,
Violet, amaracus, and asphodel,
Lotos and lilies; and a wind arose,
And overhead the wandering ivy and vine,
This way and that, in many a wild festoon
Ran riot, garlanding the gnarled boughs
With bunch and berry and flower thro'
    and thro'.

"O mother Ida, harken ere I die.
On the tree-tops a crested peacock lit,
And o'er him flow'd a golden cloud, and
    lean'd
Upon him, slowly dropping fragrant dew.
Then first I heard the voice of her to
    whom
Coming thro' heaven, like a light that
    grows
Larger and clearer, with one mind the
    Gods
Rise up for reverence. She to Paris made
Proffer of royal power, ample rule
Unquestion'd, overflowing revenue
Wherewith to embellish state, 'from many
    a vale
And river-sunder'd champaign clothed
    with corn,

Or labor'd mine undrainable of ore.
Honor,' she said, 'and homage, tax and
   toll,
From many an inland town and haven
   large,
Mast-throng'd beneath her shadowing
   citadel
In glassy bays among her tallest towers.'

  "O mother Ida, harken ere I die.
Still she spake on and still she spake of
   power,
'Which in all action is the end of all;
Power fitted to the season; wisdom-bred
And throned of wisdom — from all neigh-
   bor crowns
Alliance and allegiance, till thy hand
Fail from the sceptre-staff. Such boon
   from me,
From me, heaven's queen, Paris, to thee
   king-born,
A shepherd all thy life but yet king-born,
Should come most welcome, seeing men,
   in power
Only, are likest Gods, who have attain'd
Rest in a happy place and quiet seats
Above the thunder, with undying bliss
In knowledge of their own supremacy.'

  "Dear mother Ida, harken ere I die.
She ceased, and Paris held the costly fruit
Out at arm's-length, so much the thought
   of power
Flatter'd his spirit; but Pallas where
   she stood
Somewhat apart, her clear and bared
   limbs
O'erthwarted with the brazen-headed
   spear
Upon her pearly shoulder leaning cold,
The while, above, her full and earnest
   eye
Over her snow-cold breast and angry
   cheek
Kept watch, waiting decision, made reply:
'Self-reverence, self-knowledge, self-con-
   trol,
These three alone lead life to sovereign
   power.
Yet not for power (power of herself
Would come uncall'd for) but to live by
   law,
Acting the law we live by without fear;
And, because right is right, to follow right
Were wisdom in the scorn of conse-
   quence.'

  "Dear mother Ida, harken ere I die.
Again she said: 'I woo thee not with
   gifts.
Sequel of guerdon could not alter me
To fairer. Judge thou me by what I am,
So shalt thou find me fairest.
                    Yet, indeed,
If gazing on divinity disrobed
Thy mortal eyes are frail to judge of
   fair,
Unbias'd by self-profit, O, rest thee sure
That I shall love thee well and cleave to
   thee,
So that my vigor, wedded to thy blood,
Shall strike within thy pulses, like a
   God's,
To push thee forward thro' a life of
   shocks,
Dangers, and deeds, until endurance
   grow
Sinew'd with action, and the full-grown
   will,
Circled thro' all experiences, pure law,
Commeasure perfect freedom.'
                "Here she ceas'd,
And Paris ponder'd, and I cried, 'O
   Paris,
Give it to Pallas!' but he heard me not,
Or hearing would not hear me, woe is me!

  "O mother Ida, many-fountain'd Ida,
Dear mother Ida, harken ere I die.
Idalian Aphrodite beautiful,
Fresh as the foam, new-bathed in Paphian
   wells,
With rosy slender fingers backward drew
From her warm brows and bosom her
   deep hair
Ambrosial, golden round her lucid throat
And shoulder; from the violets her light
   foot
Shone rosy-white, and o'er her rounded
   form
Between the shadows of the vine-bunches
Floated the glowing sunlights, as she
   moved.

  "Dear mother Ida, harken ere I die.
She with a subtle smile in her mild eyes,
The herald of her triumph, drawing nigh
Half-whisper'd in his ear, 'I promise
   thee
The fairest and most loving wife in
   Greece.'
She spoke and laugh'd; I shut my sight
   for fear;